Thomas Williams Bicknell

A Memorial of a Respectable and Respected Family

Thomas Williams Bicknell

A Memorial of a Respectable and Respected Family

ISBN/EAN: 9783337006600

Printed in Europe, USA, Canada, Australia, Japan

Cover: Foto ©Thomas Meinert / pixelio.de

More available books at **www.hansebooks.com**

THE BICKNELLS.

𝔄 𝔐emorial.

JOSHUA BICKNELL'S GENEALOGY.

1635.  1880.

A

MEMORIAL

OF A

RESPECTABLE AND RESPECTED FAMILY

AND ESPECIALLY OF

JOSHUA BICKNELL,

FARMER, REPRESENTATIVE, SENATOR, JUDGE, AND EMINENT CHRISTIAN CITIZEN:

"THE NOBLEST ROMAN OF THEM ALL."

COMPILED BY

THOMAS WILLIAMS BICKNELL.

BOSTON, MASS.:
NEW-ENGLAND PUBLISHING CO., PRINTERS.
1880.

PREFACE.

To know one's ancestry is both a duty and a pleasure. Especially is this true when the line of descent is marked by men and women of integrity, virtue, manly self-reliance, and Christian deeds. Of the Bicknell family, it is quite remarkable that, while few of its members have amassed great wealth, or have achieved great names among the world's greater lights, there have been but few, if any, instances where persons have erred from the paths of honest toil and the principles of honest living before God and men. To say thus much is to confer on one's kinship a title to nobility which is essentially valuable and worthy of transmission from sire to son. I have taken great pleasure in studying my lineage to find so clear a record for all, and this little memorial of my grandfather's descent, and of his offspring, is a tribute to the labors and memories of good men and pure women.

A word or two of explanation should go out with this memorial. The first relates to the spelling of the name, Bicknell. Two spellings appear on the tombstones in Barrington, Bick*nell* and Bick*nall*, and the latter form is still in use by a few members of the family now living. That the name is *Bicknell* there can be no doubt: (1) It is the English spelling, by all of our family, past and present. (2) It was so spelled on the records of the ship Assurance. (3) It was so spelled by Zachary and John, and in the Plymouth Colony records. (4) It is so spelled invariably on the Weymouth tombstones. (5) It is so spelled by all the Weymouth Bicknells and their descendants, except in Barrington. (6) It is so spelled in the deeds and wills of most of the Barrington Bicknells. (7) It is so spelled on several of the tombstones in Barrington. (8) There are no *Bicknalls* in America that we know, except those in Barrington. (9) It is spelled Bick-*nall* and Bick*nell* by the same persons. Our conclusion s that *Bicknall* is a corruption of *Bicknell*, which has crept in by inadvertence, and has become lithographed on the tomb-stones by persons who were not aware of the correct spell-ing, or who attached no real importance to its correctness.

The Barrington Bicknells came from Weymouth between 1703 and 1706, Zachary [2] being the pioneer in the Westward migration. He settled in Swanzey, Mass. That portion of the old town in which he settled became Barrington, Mass., in 1717. and so remained until 1747, when it was joined with Warren, and was styled Warren, R. I., as the territory was then ceded by Massachusetts to Rhode Island. In 1770, Barrington became a separate township, and so remains until this day as Barrington, R. I.

OUR DESCENT.

Generation.

    I. ZACHARY and AGNES, Weymouth, Mass., 1635.

   II. JOHN and MARY (PORTER), Weymouth, Mass.

  III. ZACHARY and HANNAH (SMITH), Weymouth, Swan-zey, and Barrington, Mass.

  IV. JOSHUA and HANNAH (LYON), Barrington, R. I.

   V. JOSHUA and JERUSHA (PECK) (HEATH), Warren, R.I., and Barrington.

  VI. JOSHUA and AMY (BROWN), Barrington, R. I.

 VII. MARY, ALLEN, JOSHUA, JAMES, ELIZABETH, JOSEPH PECK.

VIII. Their children.

  IX. Their children.

   X. MABEL W. SHAW, of Attleboro, Mass. The ~~only person of the~~ 10th generation from Zachary, in the Barrington line of Bicknells.

INDEX.

THE BICKNELLS.

JOSHUA BICKNELL'S GENEALOGY.

The ship "Assurance de Lo." (*i. e.*, of London), sailed for America in the spring of 1635, from Gravesend, Kent, England, with 106 emigrants, mostly from the counties of Dorset and Somerset, in the S. W. part of England. Among these passengers were,—

1. " ZACHARY BICKNELL aged 45 yeare.
2. Agnis Bicknell his wife aged 37 yeare.
3. JN ' BICKNELL his sonne aged 11 yeare.
   Jno Kitchin his servaunt 23 yeare."

This company, under the ministerial care of Rev. Joseph Hull, settled at Weymouth, Mass., in the summer of 1635. It is probable that Mr. Bicknell died in 1636, as the General Court on the 9th of March, 1637, ordered that "William Reade, haveing bought the house & 20 acres of land at Weymouthe, vnfenced, for £7 13*s* 4*p*, wch. was Zachary Bicknels (after Bicknels death) of Richrd Rocket & his wife, is to have the same sale confirmed by the child when hee cometh to age, or else the child to alow all such costs as the Court shall think meet."

Agnes Bicknell, the widow of Zachary, married Richard Rocket (now Rockwood), of Braintree, by whom she had one child, also named John, born Dec. 1, 1641, and the ancestor of a large portion of the Rockwood family in New England. Agnes died in Braintree, July 9, 1643, aged 45 years.

3. John, the only son of Zachary and Agnes, became
an important and useful man in the town of Weymouth.
He was a selectman for many years, a deputy in the
General Court for 1677 and 1678, and died in 1679.   In
1661 he was appointed one of a committee to repair the
meeting-house (the Old North).   The town record reads
thus : "Bro Bicknell for making the meeting house
tite, 3 pounds."   He married [1] Mary ———.   They
had three children :

4. John, b. 165$\frac{3}{4}$, the first male Bicknell born in
America ; d. Aug. 4, 1737, aged 83.

5. Mary, b. ———;   m. John Dyer ; d. 167$\frac{7}{8}$.

6. Naomi, b. June 21, 1657.

His first wife, Mary, died Mar. 25, 1658.   Dec. 2,
1658, he married, for his second wife, Mary Porter, dau.
of Richard Porter, of Weymouth.   She gave birth to
eight children.

7. Ruth, b. Oct. 26, 1660 ; m. James Richards ; d.
Feb. 12, 1728.

8. Joanna, b. March 2, 1663.

9. Experience, b. Oct. 20, 1665.

10. Zachary, b. Feb. 7, 1668.

11. Thomas, b. Aug. 27, 1670 ; m. Ann Turner, at
Hingham, Feb. 16, 1696 ; removed to Middleboro ; d.
Feb. 17, 1718.

12. Elizabeth, b. Apr. 29, 1673.

13. Hannah, b. Nov. 15, 1675.

14. Mary, b. Mar. 15. 1678 ; m. Maurice Truphant,
of Weymouth ; she died Oct. 13, 1764.

10. Zechariah (Zachary), son of John and Mary
was born Feb. 7, 1668, and married Hannah Smith,
sister of Joshua Smith, of Swanzey, Nov. 24, 1692.
They lived at Weymouth, and removed to Swanzey,

Mass. (now Barrington, R. I.), about 1705, where he died. Their children were,—

15. Zechariah, b. Jan. 9, 1695, in Weymouth; went to Ashford, Conn.

16. JOSHUA, b. 1696, in Weymouth.

17. Hannah, b. Mar. 16, 1698, in Weymouth.

18. James, b. May 13, 1702, in Weymouth.

19. Mary, b. Aug. 21, 1703, in Weymouth.

20. Peter, b. ———, 1706, in Barrington; died in B. Dec. 21, 1768.

"Zachary" was a leading man in the old town of Swanzey. In the year 1711 he, with twenty - eight others, petitioned the General Court to make a new town "on the westward end of Swansea"; and in November, 1717, upon the petition of Josiah Torrey, Z. Bicknell, and Samuel Humphrey, agents, Phebe's Neck and New Meadow Neck "were erected into a township by the name of Barrington." Mr. Bicknell's house stood near the location of the Remington tavern, north of the Congregational church and fronting on the Barrington river. Town meetings were held at his house, and the town records show him to have been a valuable citizen in civil and in religious affairs.

16. JOSHUA, son of Zechariah and Hannah, b. 1696; married [1] Hannah Lyon, March 29, 1721. Hannah died Jan 25, 1737, aged 40. Children :

21. JOSHUA, b. 1723; d. Nov. 23, 1781, in 59th year.

22. Hannah, b. 1724; m. May 26, 1743, Jonathan Padelford, of Taunton, Mass.

23. Olive, ———.

24. Molly, bap. Jan. 11, 1736.

16. JOSHUA married [?] Abigail, dau. of Thomas and Anne Allen, Aug. 29, 1709. Child :

25. Allin, born July 19, 1743; d. Oct. 1, 1743.

JOSHUA died Feb. 6, 1752, in his 57th year, and his wife Abigail, Nov. 26, 1772, in her 64th year. Joshua probably lived in the house occupied by his father, with his large estate on the west and south of his residence He gave to the Congregational Church in Barrington the land on which the church now stands, and was instrumental in the erection of the new meeting-house about 1735-40. A few graves of the Bicknell family are on the farm once owned by Zechariah and Joshua, but the mounds are now entirely effaced. It is quite probable that Zechariah and some of his family were buried in this family burial-lot. Joshua and his wives were buried at Prince's Hill. His will, made Jan. 23, 1750, mentions his wife Abigail and the above-named children (except Allen). The inventory of his goods and chattels amounted to £6324, 14s. 8p., a large personal estate.

JOSHUA BICKNELL'S WILL.

JANUARY 23, 1750.

In the name of God, Amen.

I Joshua Bicknell of Warren, in the County of Bristol, in the Colony of Rhode Island in New England, being in a comfortable measure of health and memory, thanks be given to God for it; calling to mind my frailty and mortality, and that it is appointed for men once to die, do make and ordain this my Last Will and Testament; that is to say principally and first of all I give and recommend my soul into the hands of God who gave it, hoping for the pardon of all my sins and a resurrection to eternal life for the merits sake of my only Saviour Jesus Christ; and my body I commit to the earth to be decently buried at the discretion of my executrix hereinafter named; and as touching my wordly estate wherewith it hath pleased God to bless me, I give and bequeath in the manner following :

Imprimis; my will is that my just debts and funeral

charges be seasonably paid by my executrix hereinafter named.

Item. I give and bequeath to my beloved wife Abigail one third part of my real estate during her natural life. and after the payment of the legacy to my daughter Hannah hereinafter to be mentioned, I give to my said wife one third of my personal estate : And my will is that my negro man Dick and female negro child Rose in case their lives shall be spared, they shall serve my said wife during the term of her natural life, and at her decease the said two negroes shall be made free, and my said wife for this their said service shall take effectual care that they be not a charge to my children. And my will is that the other two thirds of my personal or moveable estate shall be equally divided between my son Joshua Bicknell and my two daughters, viz : Olive Bicknell and Molly Bicknell at my decease.

Item. I give and bequeath to my son Joshua Bicknell a third part of my lands adjoining to that I have already given him in Warren and one third part of my salt meadow and one hundred acres of land in Ashford. •

Item. I give and bequeath to my daughter Olive Bicknell one half third part of my lands and buildings in the town of Warren.

Item. I give and bequeath to my daughter Molly Bicknell one half third part of my lands and buildings in the town of Warren.

Item. I give to my daughter Hannah, the wife of Jonathan Padelford, seven hundred pounds old tenor to be paid by my executrix in one year after my decease.

Item. My will is in case the two negroes above mentioned should survive their mistress my said wife, that my daughter Olive shall pay the sum of one hundred pounds to the one, and my daughter Molly shall pay one hundred pounds to the other; and in case one of these negroes shall die before their mistress, then the hundred pounds to be paid by the two daughters.

Item. I give and bequeath to my son Joshua Bicknell and to my two daughters, viz: Olive Bicknell and Molly Bick-

nell after my wife's decease equally one third part of my real
estate. and in case either or both these daughters, viz : Olive
or Molly shall die without issue, my will is that all that is
given to them in this my last will and testament shall be
equally divided among my other surviving children.   And I
do nominate, constitute and appoint my wife Abigail the sole
executrix of this my last Will and Testament.

In witness whereof I have hereunto set my hand and seal
this twenty-third day of January, in the twenty-third year
of his majesty's reign. George the Second, &c., King, &c.,
Anno Domino, 1749/50.

JOSHUA BICKNELL.   { SEAL. }

Signed, Sealed, Published, &
Declared by the said Joshua
Bicknell to be his Last Will
and Testament, in presence of
us witnesses.
   John Brayley,
   Eunice Torrey,
   Solomon Townsend.

Bristol ss. Warren, March ye 2d, A.D. 1752.   Then before the Hon'ble Town Council of s'd Warren came Solomon Townsend and John Brayley, two of the witnesses to
the Last Will and Testament of Joshua Bicknell above
named. late of said Warren, deceased, and made oath that
they were present and did see and hear the s'd deceased.
sign. seal, publish, and declare the same to be his Last Will
and Testament and that he was of a sound disposing mind
when he so did, and they together with Eunice Torrey signed
in the presence of the testator.

John Kinnicut, *Council Clerk.*

———

INVENTORY.

The Inventory of goods and chattels of Mr. Joshua Bicknell, Mar. ye 2d , 1752, was taken by Matthew Allen and
Peter Bicknal, and amounted to £6324 .. 14 .. 8 deducting

Charges and Legacy £1100. Remaining to be divided, £5224 .. 14 .. 8,

whereof the widow's thirds is £1741 .. 11 .. 6.

The other two thirds we divided as followeth

To Joshua Bicknal,	£1161 .. 1 .. 2
" Olive Bicknal,	1161 .. 1 .. 0
" Molly Bicknal,	1161 .. 1 .. 0

JOHN ADAMS, JOHN KINNICUT, SOLOMON PECK.

21. JOSHUA BICKNELL, son of Joshua and Hannah, b. in Barrington, 1723; married,[1] in 1745, Ruth Bicknell, probably the dau. of James and Ruth Bicknell. She was b. 1728, and baptized July 20, 1729. The "intention of marriage" was filed Feb. 16, 1745. Ruth, his wife,[1] d. Sept. 18, 1756, in her 29th year. Children, by first marriage :

26. Thomas, b. Feb. 11, 1747.

27. James, b. Feb. 2, 1749.

28. Hannah, b, Sept. 4, 1750.

29. Ruth, b. Oct. 29, 1752.

30. Olive, b. Nov. 11, 1754 ; m. Joseph C. Mauran.

21. JOSHUA married [2] in 1758, Mrs. Jerusha Heath, widow of Rev. Peleg Heath. Jerusha was the dau. of Joseph and Rebecca (Brown) Peck, b. Nov. 18, 1724, and married [1] Rev. Peleg Heath ; she died Apr. 9, 1763, in her 39th year. Children by second marriage :

31. JOSHUA, b. Jan. 14, 1759 ; d. Dec. 16, 1837, aged 78.

32. Winchester, b. Mar. 31, 1761 ; d. July 20, 1782, aged 21.

33. Jerusha ⎫ twins, b.   ⎰ d. Mar. 13, 1763.

34. Joseph ⎭ Jan. 20, 1763. ⎱ d Jan 19, 1848, aged 85.

21. JOSHUA married,[3] in 1764, Hannah ———, b. 1727.

35. Hannah,[3] with her infant child, died Aug. 11, 1765, in her 39th year.

21. JOSHUA married[4] in 1767, Freeborn ———,
b. 1728.   Children by fourth marriage:

36. Freeborn, b. Jan. 9, 1768; m. Aug. 16, 1787,
Thomas Baker.

37. Wait, b. Nov. 9, 1771 ; d. Apr. 9, 1773.

JOSHUA died suddenly, Nov. 30, 1781, in his 59th year.
On the 3d of Dec. of that year his son Joshua appeared
before the Town Council of Barrington and requested
letters of administration on the estate of his father, who
died intestate.   The widow, Mrs. Freeborn Bicknell,
was allowed such furniture out of her husband's inventory as was necessary for the term of her natural life.
She married again, at the age of 72, Feb. 24, 1799, Mr.
Barnard Miller, of Warren, then aged 79, the ceremony
being performed by Rev. Samuel Watson.   She died,
as may be seen by the tombstone near her husband's
grave, on the 1st of Feb., 1820, aged 93.

33. WINCHESTER BICKNELL, son of Joshua, entered
the Revolutionary Marine service, and was on board
the privateer "Chance," Captain Dring, when she was
captured by a British cruiser off Long Island, May 11,
1782.   Captain Dring, in his narrative of the capture
and imprisonment, speaks of young Bicknell as follows :

"The prisoners were put on board the Jersey, May 19,
and were released after a close imprisonment of two months,
during which time seventeen had died, and nearly all the
others were dangerously sick of disease contracted on that
loathsome prison-ship.   One of our number who was thus
seized by the fever was a young man named Bicknell, of
Barrington, R. I.   He was unwell when we left the Jersey,
and his symptoms indicated the approaching fever; and
when we entered Narragansett Bay, he was apparently dy-
ing.   Being informed that we were in the Bay, he begged to

be taken on deck, or at least to the hatchway, that he might look once more upon his native land. He said that he was sensible of his condition ; that the hand of death was upon him ; but that he was consoled by the thought that his remains would be decently interred and be suffered to rest among those of his friends and kindred. I was astonished at the degree of resignation and composure with which he spoke. He pointed to his father's house as we approached it, and said that it contained all that was dear to him on earth. He requested to be put on shore. Our captain was intimately acquainted with the family of the sufferer, and as the wind was light, we dropped our anchor and complied with his request. He was placed in the boat, where I took a seat by his side in order to support him, and with two boys at the oars we left the sloop. In a few minutes his strength began rapidly to fail. He laid his fainting head upon my shoulder, and said he was going to the shore to be buried with his ancestors ; that this had long been his ardent desire, and that God had heard his prayers. No sooner had we touched the shore, than one of the boys was sent to inform his family of the event. They hastened to the boat to receive their long-lost son and brother; but we could only give them,—his yet warm but lifeless corpse."

In the poem, " An Hundred Golden Years," read at the Barrington Centennial, June 17, 1870, Mr. Butterworth refers to Winchester Bicknell as follows :

> " I need not tell you that they fought
>   The Jerseys' hills among,
> I need not speak of *him* they brought,
>   When life was fresh and young,
> From strife upon the periled seas
>   To die upon the bay
> Hard by the shade of native trees,
>   Some fourscore years to-day."

31. Joshua Bicknell b. Jan. 14, 1759 ; m. Amy

BROWN, Apr. 19, 1782 ; d. Dec. 16, 1837, in his 79th year.

CHILDREN.

38. Jerusha Bicknell, b. Mar. 5, 1783 ; d. Sept. 25, 1857.

39. MARY BICKNELL, b. Nov. 19, 1784 ; d. July 19, 1866.

40. ALLIN BICKNELL, b. Apr. 13, 1787 ; d. Aug. 22, 1870.

41. Amy Bicknell, b. Aug. 15, 1789 ; d. July 26, 1877.

42. Freeborn Bicknell, b. Nov. 5, 1791 ; d. Nov. 22, 1791.

43. JOSHUA BICKNELL, b. Nov. 19, 1792 ; d. Feb. 19, 1821.

44. JAMES BICKNELL, b. Nov. 4, 1795.

45. ELIZABETH BICKNELL, b. Feb. 22, 1799.

46. JOSEPH PECK BICKNELL, b. Apr. 19, 1801.

31. JOSHUA BICKNELL [6] (Zachary, [1] John, [2] Zechariah, [3] Joshua, [4] Joshua, [5]) was born at the house known as The Kinnicutt Tavern, in Barrington, Jan. 14. 1759. His education was limited to the district school instruction of the olden time, and comprehended the rudiments of arithmetic, reading, spelling, and writing. Amy Brown, his wife, was born at " The Ferry House," then owned by Col. Nathaniel Martin, opposite Warren, Aug. 1. 1762. They were married April 18, 1782, by Rev. Solomon Townsend, the venerable minister of Barrington, and went to house-keeping in his father's house, on the spot where The Remington Tavern stood. Here Jerusha was born, after which they moved into the Conet house, afterwards owned by Martin Brown, which stood on the site of the residence of Royal D. Horton. Here Mary and Allin were born, after which Joshua built the house in which he afterwards lived, and now owned and occupied by his son, Joseph Peck Bicknell. Here the other children were born.

Born and bred to a farmer's life, JOSHUA BICKNELL made a good use of the limited educational privileges of his day, and by reason of fine natural abilities, energy, and integrity, became a useful man and an honored citizen. He entered public life when but a youth, and throughout his career served the town, county, and State, in various official positions. He was a senator or a representative in the General Assembly of Rhode Island in 1787, '88, '89, '90, '91, '92, '93, '94, '96, '97 and '98 ; 1802, '03, and '04 ; 1807, and '08 ; 1823, '24, and '25. He served as an Associate Justice of the Supreme Court of Rhode Island from 1794 to 1837. The purity of his life, the integrity of his motives, and the justice of his opinions and decisions gave him the merited soubriquet of " Old Aristides." He was plain in his domestic habits, and while unoccupied with public affairs, devoted himself to his farm, and especially to fruit-culture, in which he took great pleasure. He united with the Congregational Church in Barrington, Nov. 5, 1805, and held the office of Deacon for many years. He was also Treasurer of the United Congregational Society from its formation in 1797, till his death in 1837, a period of forty years. The following obituary appeared in the *Providence Journal* at his death :

OBITUARY.

Died at Barrington on Saturday last, Hon. Joshua Bicknell, aged 79, for many years a distinguished Justice of the Supreme Court of Rhode Island. He was early and repeatedly a member of the General Assembly, and survived all who were members with him when he first took his seat, excepting two. He has also filled various other public offices by special appointment, with distinguished ability.

But very few men have been better known through the
State, and perhaps none survived him who possess more
historical and statistical knowledge of the State from the
commencement of the Revolution to the present time.   Of
no man may it be more justly said, he has lived devoted to
the best interests of Rhode Island.   No man more ardently
loved his country.   Respecting his talents and acquirements,
—he read much, meditated much; but perhaps the most
wonderful trait in his character was his extraordinary power
of discrimination.   In these particulars he has left few su-
periors, even among those more fortunate in opportunities
for improvement.   But that which adds the brightest luster
to his character is that his latter days have especially adorned
the Christian character.   The church of which he was a
member, and in which he had long sustained an important
office, have great reason to mourn that a good and distinguished man in Israel has fallen.

39. MARY BICKNELL m. to Rev. Seth Chapin, of
Mendon, Mass., a graduate of Brown University, and
at that time a student at Andover Theological Sem-
inary, on the 27th of May, 1810, by Rev. Samuel Watson,
of Barrington.

CHILDREN.

47. Joshua Bicknell Chapin, b. Aug. 19, 1812, Hills-
boro, N. H.

48. Moses Thompson Chapin, b. April, 1814, Hills-
boro, N. H.; d. Irvington, Ala., Sept. 11, 1836.

Moses T. Chapin was a young man of great promise,
and, on leaving Williams College, studied law for one
year with Samuel Ames, since Chief Justice of the Supreme Court of Rhode Island.   He then went to Savannah, Ga., and thence to Columbus, where he com-
menced the practise of law.   He then took up his
residence at Irvington, Ala., where he died of bilious

fever, September 11, 1836. His remains rest in that place.

40. ALLIN BICKNELL married[1] Harriet Byron Kinnicutt, of Barrington, Dec. 23, 1817 ; b. Sept. 1, 1791 ; d. Dec. 15, 1837. Married[2] Elizabeth W. Allen, of Barrington ; she died in Barrington, Oct. 16, 1868, aged 81 years. He died Aug. 16, 1870, aged 83 years.

CHILDREN.

49. Joshua, b. Oct. 29, 1818.

50. George Augustus, b. June 30, 1822 ; d. July 21, 1861.

51. Daniel Kinnicutt, b. Sept 24, 1829; d. August 26, 1851.

52. Thomas Williams, b. Sept. 6, 1834.

ALLIN BICKNELL, son of Joshua and Amy, born April 13, 1787, was brought up in, and devoted himself to a farmer's life. He joined the Congregational Church in Barrington, with about seventy others, following the great revival, in June, 1820, and maintained a consistent Christian character for more than fifty years. He succeeded his honored father, Judge Bicknell, as a deacon of the Congregational Church, and held the office till his death. He held various offices in the town, was a member of the town council for several years, was a representative of the town in the General Assembly for the years 1842, '46, '49, and a senator for the years 1850, '51, '52, '53. He married, for his first wife, Harriet Byron Kinnicutt, daughter of Josiah and Rebecca Kinnicutt, and lived during her life on the farm which was Joseph Bicknell's (now owned by the Tiffanys), near the Congregational church. After his marriage with Elizabeth W. Allen, daughter of Gen. Thomas and Amy Allen, he moved to her farm at Drownville, and lived in the General Allen house. He was industrious in habit, generous, hospitable, entertaining many ministerial as well as other guests. He died triumphing in the true faith, Monday, Aug. 22, 1870, aged 83 years, 4 months, and 7 days, and was buried with his fathers at Prince's Hill Cemetery. The following obituary notice, written by Rev. Rufus Babcock, D.D., his early and life-long friend, appeared in the *Providence Journal*, soon after his death:

THE LATE ALLEN BICKNELL, OF BARRINGTON.

This venerable man, this good and honored citizen, who has just fallen asleep at the ripe age of four score and three years,— the oldest man in town,— is eminently deserving of some special notice. The son of Judge Joshua and Amy Bicknell, he was born in Barrington, April 13, 1787, and married to Harriet Byron Kinnicutt, December 23, 1817, by Rev. Luther Wright. Four sons were born to them between 1818 and 1834,—Joshua, George, Daniel, and Thomas. Harriet, his first wife, died Dec. 15, 1837, of consumption, aged 46 years. He married Elizabeth Walden Allen, April 13, 1839, who died without issue, Oct. 16, 1868, aged 81 years. Allen Bicknell experienced renewing grace during the "Great Revival" in Barrington, in the winter of 1819–20, and with about seventy others, united with the Congregational Church in June, 1820. For more than fifty years he maintained a consistent Christian walk and conversation, and in many trying periods in the history of the church he helped to defend the Ark of the Lord. The truths of the Bible were his comfort, strength, and delight, and in its precepts he meditated day and night. His prayers were gifted and importunate; his exhortations earnest and Scriptural; and the accurate, apt quotations of Scripture, with his frequent reference to Scripture history, showed him to be a good Bible student.

The church and the town both honored him with many tokens of their confidence. He succeeded his honored father, Judge Bicknell, in 1839, as deacon of the church, an office which he held until his death. Various offices in the town were also confided to him. For several years he was chosen to represent the people in both branches of the Legislature, and performed these duties in a manner highly acceptable and useful. But public life was by no means his choice. His honest integrity, and his quiet, unobtrusive, healthy tone of life rendered him the admiration and delight of the private circle, where, without ostentatious parade or pretentiousness of any kind, he won the full confidence and esteem of those most intimate with him. His prudent and temperate care, in the exercise of godly virtues, bore him on the even tenor of his way, and carried him beyond the bounds of four-score years. Delightful was the privilege of those admitted to intimate intercourse with him, on his death-bed. It seemed like the days of heaven upon earth, so full of blessed resignation to his Heavenly Father's will, so buoyed up with hopes of soon being reunited with the many he had loved on earth; and, above all, so filled with joyous anticipation of meeting his adored Saviour. Like the morning star, which goes not down, nor hides beyond the darkening west, but melts away into the light of heaven,— so bright, pure, peaceful was his departure, August 22, 1870. Devout men carried him to the grave, after impressive and interesting services in the church, where the pastor, Rev. Mr. Horton, and a former pastor, Rev. Mr. Wood, and his venerable, early friend, Rev. Dr. Shepard, of Bristol, officiated.

43. JOSHUA BICKNELL married Elizabeth Marchant Sessions (b. at Newport, R. I., Aug. 5, 1792), May 21 1817.

CHILDREN (*all born at Providence*).

53. Zechariah, b. May 4, 1818 ; d. in infancy.

54. Edward Joshua, b. Oct. 13, 1819.

55. Amy Elizabeth, b. Mar. 30, 1821 ; d. Jan. 12, 1841.

On the family burial-lot at the North Burial-ground, Providence, R. I., is a monument with this inscription :

"JOSHUA BICKNALL, JR.,
Born in
Barrington, R. I.,
Nov. 19, 1792.
Died at Balize,
Mexico,
Feby. 19th, 1821."

JOSHUA BICKNELL, son of Joshua and Amy, was born at Barrington, R. I., Nov. 19, 1792. He left home at the age of 16 years, and engaged with Deacon Walter Paine, of Providence, R. I., as clerk. Having served his time, he was received as partner at the age of 21 years. He remained with Mr. Paine some two years, when he left the business and went to Savannah, Ga., on his own account. After a short sojourn he returned to Providence, and formed a business connection with Darius Sessions, under the firm name of Bicknell & Sessions, which continued with a fair share of success until his death. A portion of the business of the house was trading between Providence and the Spanish Main, which at times required the presence of Joshua at the other end of the line ; and it was on one of these trips,—having gone out in one of their trading vessels,—that he was seized with fever at Balize, Mexico, from which he died. His widow, now in her 89th year, is in very fair health, and her mental faculties are wonderfully preserved. Her paternal grandfather was the last Colonial Governor of Rhode Island, and her maternal grandfather was Henry Marchant, of Newport, an eminent lawyer of his day, and the first district judge appointed under General Washington.

44. JAMES BICKNELL, born Nov. 4, 1795, seafarer, in which he rose to the position of mate, and sailed between American, European, and Asiatic ports ; afterward farmer. He married,[1] Dec. 21, 1829, Elizabeth Scott Short, b. Jan. 25, 1808. Children by first marriage :

56. Olive Humphrey, b. July 27, 1831.

57. Harriet Atwood, b. Jan. 11, 1836.

James married [2] April 15, 1858, Miss Fanny Maria Daggett, b. Oct. 16, 1815, and both are now living on their farm in East Providence, R. I.

45. ELIZABETH BICKNELL, born Feb. 22, 1799 ; married Anson Viall, March 29, 1832. Anson Viall, born April 9, 1795 ; occupation, farmer ; died Nov. 3, 1866.

CHILDREN.

58. Mary, b. Feb. 13, 1833.

59. Richmond, b. Dec. 16, 1834.

60. Amy Brown, b. March 12, 1836.

61. Nathaniel, b. April 1, 1838 ; d. June 10, 1856.

62. Elizabeth Bicknell, b. Sept. 29, 1842.

46. JOSEPH PECK BICKNELL, b. Apr. 19, 1801 ; farmer, and lives in the house built and occupied by his father, Joshua ; married Louisa Allen (b. Aug. 15, 1801), dau. of Capt. Samuel Allen, of Seekonk (now East Providence), Dec. 5, 1827.

CHILDREN.

63. Henry, b. Aug. 29, 1828.

64. George Freeman, b. May 4, 1830.

65. Louisa, A. b. March 2, 1836 ; m. Otis Harris.

49. JOSHUA BICKNELL, b. Oct. 29, 1818; carpenter and marketman; m. Esther Peck Viall (b. March 29, 1819), Nov. 28, 1844; residence, Providence, R. I.

CHILDREN.

66. Harriet Kinnicutt, b. May 2, 1846.
67. Walter Joshua, b. Jan. 27, 1848.
68. Daniel Bicknell, b. Aug. 10, 1851; d. Sept. 24, 1853.

50. GEORGE AUGUSTUS BICKNELL, b. June 30, 1822; farmer, drover, and marketman; residence, Springfield, Mass.; m.[1] Margaret Jane Thompson (born at Wales, Mass., July 15, 1829), Sept. 24, 1848; she d. Oct. 5, 1856.

CHILDREN.

69. George A. Bicknell, Jr., b. Oct. 11, 1851; d. Dec. 3, 1853.
70. George Henry Bicknell, b. Feb. 1, 1853.
71. Emma Elizabeth Bicknell, b. May 14, 1855.

GEORGE A. BICKNELL, m.[2] Elizabeth Oliver (b. May 16, 1827), Aug. 26, 1857.

CHILDREN.

72. Harriet Jane, b. May 26, 1858; d Nov. 16, 1879.
73. Annetta Louisa, b. May 13, 1859; d. Aug. 6, 1859.
74. Ella Amy, b. Oct. 26, 1860.
75. Frederick Augustus, b. Feb. 27, 1862.

George A. Bicknell died, at Springfield, July 21, 1861.

52. THOMAS WILLIAMS, named for Rev. Thomas Williams (b. Sept. 6, 1834); m. Sept. 5, 1860, Amelia Davie Blanding, dau. of Christopher and Chloe Blanding, Rehoboth, Mass.

CHILD.

76. Martha Elizabeth, b. Oct. 10, 1862 ; d. Sept. 17, 1867 ; age 4 yrs. 11 mos. 7 days.

THOMAS W. received his early education in district and private schools in Barrington until sixteen years of age, when he left home to attend school at Thetford Academy, Vt., living in the family and working the farm of Enoch Slade, Esq. While at the Academy, under the very efficient principalship and instruction of Hiram Orcutt, he decided to take the studies preparatory for college, and in 1853 graduated from the Academy, delivering the Greek oration on Grecian Mythology. Taught his first school at Seekonk, Mass., 1853–4. Admitted by examination to Dartmouth and Amherst Colleges, and entered the Freshman class of Amherst, Sept. 1853. At the close of Freshman year he was elected by his class as a prize-debater, and became a member of the *A. A. Φ.* fraternity. Left college in 1854, to recruit in health and funds. Taught school as principal of the public school and high school, Rehoboth, Mass., 1854–5. Went West in 1855, and taught as principal of the academy at Elgin Ill. In the summer of 1856 joined a Chicago emigration company to settle in Kansas. Taken prisoner by border ruffians on Missouri River, and sent back to St. Louis under escort of Colonel Bufford's South Carolina and Virginia Sharpshooters.

Came East and conducted Rehoboth High School from Sept., 1856, to Dec., 1857. Entered Sophomore class of Brown University, Feb., 1858. Graduated with degree of A.M., 1860. Was principal of Bristol High School, from May, 1860, to Feb., 1863 ; principal of Arnold Street Grammar School, Providence, 1863 to 1867, till the school was closed ; returned to principalship of Bristol High School, and resigned May, 1869. Ap-

pointed Commissioner of Public Schools of Rhode
Island, by Governor Padelford, June, 1869, and continued in office till Jan. 1, 1875. While Commissioner,
secured a State Board of Education, of which he
was Secretary; the reëstablishment of the State Nor-
mal School; the reëstablishment of *The Rhode Island
Schoolmaster*, of which he was EDITOR for nearly ten
years; secured town school superintendents in each
town in the State; dedicated over fifty new school-
houses; advanced the school-year from 27 to 35 weeks
average throughout the State; and school appropria-
tions were nearly trebled during his administration.
Aided in the revival of the American Institute of Instruction, and in the establishment of the NEW-ENGLAND
JOURNAL OF EDUCATION, and as joint proprietor and
publisher with C. C. Chatfield, edited THE JOURNAL,
which united the several monthly magazines of New
England in one paper, issued weekly at Boston, Mass.
Established and edited THE PRIMARY TEACHER, a
monthly magazine, in 1876. In 1880 established and
became conductor of EDUCATION, a bimonthly Review
on the Science, the Art, the Philosophy, and the History of Education; at the same time continuing the ed-
itorship of THE JOURNAL and Presidency of the New-
England Publishing Company, formed in 1875. His
present business is that of editing and publishing educational papers, books, and magazines.

He was a member of the School Board and Superintendent of Schools, and a member of the Town Council
of Barrington, R. I., for several years; president of the
Rhode Island Institute of Instruction for the years
1867–8; president of the American Institute of Instruction 1877 and 1878, with meetings at Montpelier, Vt.,
and at Fabyans, White Mountains, N. H. As a result of

the latter meeting, a fund of one thousand dollars was created, called THE BICKNELL FUND, and money was raised to build the mountain-path up Mt. Carrigan, N. H. ; was partly instrumental in the formation of the National Council of Education, and was elected its first president at Chautauqua, July, 1880.

He engaged in religious work in 1851 at Thetford, and joined the Congregational Church while at the Academy. Was superintendent of the Sunday-school at Bristol, R. I., 1861 to 1864 ; of the Sunday-school at Barrington, from 1864 to 1875 ; and of the Second Church Sunday-school, Dorchester, Boston, 1876 to 1880. Aided in the formation of the Boston Congregational Sunday-school Superintendents Union, and was elected its president May, 1880. Was a delegate to and attended the Raikes Sunday-school Centenary at London, 1880. He has lectured, and given addresses in various parts of the country. Delivered the oration at the centennial of his native town, Barrington, June 17, 1870. His published works are, *A Memorial of William Lord Noyes*, 1868 ; *A History of Barrington*, 1870; Reports as Commissioner of Public Schools, 1870, '71, '72, '73, '74 ; an Address on School Supervision, 1876 ; with editorial and other articles in *Rhode Island Schoolmaster*, JOURNAL OF EDUCATION, and other publications.

He is a member of the Massachusetts Historic Genealogical Society, of the Rhode Island Historical Society, of the American Association for the Advancement of Science, of the American Social Science Association, and an honorary member of the Pennsylvania Historical Society. The Bicknell Family Association was formed in Boston in December, 1879, and Mr. Bicknell was elected its president. He is also a member of various other social, historic, and religious organizations. In 1872 he was elected an honorary member of the Φ. B. K., and received the honorary degree of Master of Arts from Amherst College in 1880.

Mr. Bicknell was President of the R. I. Sunday-school Union from 1872 to 1875 ; was a delegate from the Rhode Island Conference to form the National Congregational Council, and was a delegate from the Suffolk South Conference to the Triennial Council, held in Detroit, Mich., Oct., 1877 ; was Commissioner from R. I. to the Universal Exposition at Vienna, Austria, in 1873, and a member of the Postal Congress held in New York, 1878, in forming the Postal Code, adopted by Congress in 1879.

In political life Mr. Bicknell has held several prominent positions, the chief of which was Representative to the General Assembly of Rhode Island, to which he was elected by the citizens of Barrington while he was a Junior in Brown University. In that legislature he made an elaborate speech in favor of the union of colored and white schools in the State.

Mr. Bicknell has traveled extensively through the United States, and has made three European trips. In 1873 he traveled through Scotland, England, France, Holland, Belgium, Switzerland, Italy, Greece, Turkey, Austria, and Bavaria. In 1879 he revisited England, and in 1880, with his wife, visited Scotland, England, France, Belgium, and Holland. Cast his first Presidential vote for John C. Fremont, in 1856, and still holds fast to the Republican party.

54. EDWARD JOSHUA was born Oct. 13, 1819 ; merchant and cotton broker, Providence, R. I.; was married to Eleanor Proctor Najac, Oct. 18, 1840. She was born at Providence, R. I., Apr. 25, 1821.

CHILDREN.

77. Edward, b. Mar. 18, 1842 ; merchant.

78. Frank Joshua, b. Feb. 14, 1845 ; merchant.

54. EDWARD JOSHUA, after the death of his father, was reared by his grandfather Bicknell, at Barrington. At the age of 15 years, he left home for Providence, serving his time with the late Seth Adams, Jr., where he obtained his business education. After leaving Mr. Adams, he was for several years in the employment of the late Charles C. Mowry, who was largely engaged in mercantile and shipping business, as clerk and general manager. He left Mr. Mowry in 1851, and formed a business connection with Darius S. Skinner, under the firm name of Bicknell & Skinner, and did a very heavy and successful southern and eastern trade until reverses, caused by the memorable panic of 1857, swept away in a few days the results of all their efforts. Since then, his time has been devoted to various mercantile enterprises and real estate transactions.

56. OLIVE HUMPHREY BICKNELL, b. July 27, 1831 ; m. Lyman Hayward (b. Oct. 23, 1825), Oct. 13, 1849 ; residence, Providence, R. I.

57. HARRIET ATWOOD, b. Jan. 11, 1836 ; m. Thompson Murdock (b. Aug. 10, 1826) April 11, 1861 ; residence, Providence, R. I.

CHILDREN.

79. Infant son, b. July 26, 1867 ; d. July 29, 1867.

80. Willard Chase, b. April 11, 1873.

58. MARY VIALL, b. Feb. 13, 1833 ; m. Edward Robinson Wheeler (b. Jan. 10, 1827), June 3, 1858 ; residence, Providence, R. I.

CHILDREN.

81. Edward Bicknell, b. April 16, 1859.
82. Annie Maria, b. Oct. 8, 1860.
83. Mary Chapin, b, Sept. 30, 1861.
84. Frances Mason, b. Feb. 13, 1863.
85. Marion Elizabeth, b. June 6. 1868.
86. Horace Viall, b. May 11, 1872 ; d. June 25, 1874.
87. Emma Louise, b. May 9, 1873.

59. RICHMOND VIALL ; occupation, machinist ; married June 1, 1859, Eliza Nelson Cole, born Jan. 14, 1842.

CHILDREN.

· 88. William Angell, b. Oct. 26, 1861.
89. Richmond Irwin. b. Nov. 6, 1863; d. June 10, 1875.
90. Abert Anson Viall, b. Sept. 5, 1871.

63. HENRY BICKNELL, mechanic and jeweller, married Louisa Oliver (b. July 12, 1839, Troy, N. Y.), at Springfield, Mass., Nov. 29, 1860.   Residence, Barrington, R. I.

CHILD.

91. Mary Eleanor, b. in Springfield, Mass., Jan. 4, 1862.

64. GEORGE FREEMAN BICKNELL b. May 4, 1830, married Angenett Wilmarth, of Attleboro, Mass., Dec, 31, 1854 ; business, gold-plater ; residence, Attleboro. Mass. Enlisted as a private, was commissioned first-lieutenant in the 12th R. I. Infantry, Oct. 13, 1862 ; afterwards commissioned first-lieutenant, and was promoted to captaincy in the 3d R. I. Cavalry ; was mustered out of service June 29, 1865 ; has been junior and senior warden and master of Ezekiel Bates Lodge of F. and A. M.

CHILD.

92. Emily, b. July 18, 1859. Emily married Joseph B. Shaw, of Attleboro.

CHILD.

93. Mabel W. Shaw, b. Oct. 24, 1878.

66. HARRIET K. BICKNELL, b. May 2, 1846 ; m. Asher Huntington Young, Nov. 17, 1868 ; business, commercial traveler ; residence, Providence, R. I.

CHILD.

94. Walter Huntington Young, b. Aug. 16, 1869 ; d. May 8, 1870.

Asher H. Young died in Providence, Jan. 11, 1880.

67. WALTER J., b. Jan. 27, 1848 ; salesman and commercial traveler ; m. Mary E. Blackburn (b. March 17, 1848), June 5, 1872 ; residence, Providence, R. I.

CHILDREN.

95. Annie Isabella, b. March 25, 1874.
96. Edith May, b. June 27, 1876.
97. Grace Louise, b. March 29, 1878.

OLD INSCRIPTIONS ON TOMBSTONES,

AT WEYMOUTH, MASS.

———

[Head-stone.]

HER LYETHE BoDY
oF IoSEPH BIcKnELL
dYEd In THE 22 YER
oF HIS AgE.   1719

[Foot-stone.]

I   B

———

[Head-stone.]

HERE LYES Y^e BODY OF
Mr IOHN BICKNELL SEN^r
DEC^D AUGUST 4th
1 7 3 7
IN Y^e 84th
OF HIS AGE.

———

[Head-stone.]

HERE LIES THE
BODY OF
MARY BICKNELL
DAU^r OF M^r
EBENEZER & M^rs
MARY BICKNELL
DIED OCT^r 12th
1751 IN Y^e 16th
YEAR OF HER AGE.

THE

BICKNELLS.

—•—

INSCRIPTIONS ON TOMBSTONES,

IN BARRINGTON, R. I.

AND JACOB SET A PILLAR UPON HER GRAVE: THAT IS THE PILLAR OF RACHEL'S GRAVE UNTO THIS DAY.

GEN. XXXV.: 20.

Inscriptions on Tombstones.

The following record is intended to be a correct copy of the inscriptions on the tombstones in Barrington, of all the members of the Bicknell family-name, to whose memories stones have been erected. All but two of the graves with tombstones are at Prince's Hill. The record of Allin Bicknall, 1743, was taken from a stone in a family yard on land once owned by Joshua Bicknell and his heirs, afterwards by Enoch Remington, and now by the heirs of Mr. Charles Miller. There were several mounds in that yard which have been obliterated by the cultivation of the land. The record of Abigail Bicknall, who died 1772, was taken from a stone in the Allen burial ground at Drownville, south of the road leading to Bullock's Cove.

In Memory of
Allen Bicknall, Son
of Mr Jofhua Bicknall
& Abigail his Wife
Dec^d. Octo^r. y^9 1ft
1743, Aged 10
Weeks.

(Foot-stone.)

A. B.

In Memory of

Mr Joshua Bicknall who

Departed this Life on y^e

6th day of February Anno

Dom. 1 7 5 2

in ye 57th Year of

his Age.

—

Blessed are ye Dead who Die in ye Lord.

(Foot stone.)

Joshua
Bicknall.
1 7 5 2 .

———◆———

Here lies ye Body of

Hannah Bicknall

ye wife of Joshua

Bicknall, who depart^d

this Life June ye 25th

1737, in ye 40th Year

of her Age.

———

(Foot-stone.)

Hannah
Bicknall,
1 7 3 7

Here lieth all

that was mortal

of JOSHUA

BICKNALL Eſq

who died ſuddenly

Nov. 23^{d} 1781 in the

59 Year of his Age.

———

Foot ſtone)
     JOSHUA

BICKNALL

Eſq: 1781,

— · ——

In Memory of

M^{rs}. RUTH BICKNALL

ye wife of M^{r}· Joshua Bick-

nall who Departed this

Life Sept. 18. 1756.

in ye 29th Year of her Age.

———

Christian Reader cast an Eye,
As you are now so once was I,
As I am now so must you be,
Prepare your heart to follow me.

———

(Foot ſtone)
     RUTH

BICKNALL

1 7 5 6

In Memory of

Mrs JERUSHA

BICKNALL

late Wife of

Jofhua Bicknall Esqr

She Died April 9th.

1763 in the 39th

Year of her Age.

———

(Foot-stone.)   M^{rs}

Jerusha

Bicknall

1 7 6 3

———•———

In Memory of

Mrs HANNAH

BICKNALL

and her Infant

Child, late Wife

of Joshua Bicknall

Efq'r, Dec^d Auguft

11th 1765 in the

39 Year of her

Age.

In Memory of

Mr. WINCHESTER

BICKNALL, Son of

Jofhua Bicknall, Esq &.

Mrs Jerufha his Wife

He died July 20th,

1782, aged 21 Years

3 Months & 20 Days.

—

Alas dear Friend no fooner came,
Thy earthly ufefulnefs to Bloom,
But Death has cropt thy tender Bud,
And laid the in this mournful Tomb.

(Foot stone.)

Mr
Winchefter
Bicknall,
1 7 8 2 .

In Memory of

ABIGAIL

BICKNALL

Relict of Mr JOSHUA

BICKNALL who

departed this Life

November 26 1772

Aged 63 Years 2

Months and 26 days.

Here lieth all that

was Mortal of

Peter Bicknell Esqr.

whose Soul quitted this

earthly Tabernacle on the

21^{ft.} Day of December AD.

1768 in ye 63 Year

of his Age.

—

Nor Wealth nor Strength, nor Friends nor Parts,
Can rescue from Deaths piercing Darts,
Then mind thy Doom and passing by,
Be Wise by times prepare to die.

(Foot-stone.)

PETER
BICKNELL Efqr.
1 7 6 8 .

———

Here lieth

all that was mor-

tal of Mrs Rachel

Bicknall widow

of Peter Bicknall

Esq: who Died

December 10^{th,} 1786

in ye 75th Year

of her age.

—

Thrice happy change,
it is for me,
From Earth to Heaven,
Remov.d to be.

In memory

of Rachel Bicknall

Daugh^{tr} of Peter Bick-

nall Efq. & Mrs Rachel his

Wife, Dec^{d.} March ye 5th

1752 in ye 15th Year of

her Age.

———◆———

In Memory of

Wait Bicknall

Daught. of M^{r.}

Jofhua Bicknall

& Mrs. Freeborn

his Wife who

died April 9th 1773

aged 1 Year & 5 Months.

———

(Foot-stone.)

W * B

1773

Sacred to the memory

OF

ASA BICKNALL, Esq,

who departed this life

June 14, A.D 1799

aged 52 years.

(Foot-stone.)

Asa Bicknall, Esq.
1799.

———•———

Here lieth

all that was mor-

tal of ASA a ſon

of M^r Aſa & M^{rs}.

Elizabeth Bicknal

(1)

who Died

September 20th 17-

87 in y̆ 17 Year

of his age.

—

Betimes his Virtu-
ous race began.
But to our grief,
too soon twas done.

(Foot-stone.)   Asa
Bicknall
1787

In Memory of
Deacon
JOSHUA BICKNELL,
Born Jan. 14, 1759:
Died Dec. 16, 1837.
Aged 78.

(Foot-stone.)

J. B.

In Memory
of
MRS AMY BICKNELL,
Wife of
DEA. JOSHUA BICKNELL.
Born Aug. 1, 1762.
Died Oct. 15, 1846.
Aged 84.

(Foot-stone.)

A. B.

JERUSHA,

DAU. OF

JOSHUA & AMY

BICKNELL,

DIED SEPT. 25, 1857.

IN THE 75TH YEAR

OF HER AGE.

———

(Foot-stone.)

J. B.

———•———

AMY,

DAU. OF

JOSHUA & AMY

BICKNELL,

DIED JULY 26, 1877,

IN THE 88TH YEAR

OF HER AGE.

———

(Foot stone.)

A. B.

DEA. ALLIN BICKNELL.

Son of

DEA. JOSHUA & AMEY

BICKNELL.

Born April 13, 1787.

Died Aug. 22, 1870.

Aged 83 years.

—

With long life will I satisfy him,
and shew him my salvation.

— Ps. XCI, 16.

———•———

HARRIET B. KINNICUT,

Wife of

ALLIN BICKNELL,

died Dec. 15, 1837,

Aged 46 Years.

———

" Precious in the sight of the LORD,
is the death of his saints."

ELIZABETH W. BICKNELL,
Wife of
ALLIN BICKNELL,
and daughter of
THOMAS & AMEY ALLEN.
Born June 9, 1787.
Died Oct. 16, 1868,
Aged 81 years.

—

Rest.

———•———

DANIEL K. BICKNELL,
Son of
Allin & Harriet B.
Bicknell,
Born Sept. 24, 1829.
Died Aug. 26, 1851,
in the 22d year
of his age.

———

(Foot-stone.)

D. K. B.

DANIEL,

Son of

Joshua & Esther P.

Bicknell,

died Sept. 24, 1853,

aged 2 years, 1 mo.

& 14 days.

—

We would not call thee back to earth
But love thee still the more,
Since thou art not lost to us
But only gone before.

(Foot stone.)

D. B.

MATTIE.

(On the face.

He shall gather the lambs with his arm,
and carry them in his bosom.

Isaiah XL, 11.

(On the back.)

MATTIE E.

Daughter of

THOMAS W. AND AMELIA D.

BICKNELL.

Died Sept. 17, 1867,

Age 4 years, 11 mos,

& 7 days.

JOSEPH BICKNELL.

Born Jan. 20,

1763.

Died Jan. 19,

1848.

aged 85 years.

———

(Foot stone.)

J. B.

———•———

ALATHEA BICKNELL,

Wife of

Joseph Bicknell.

Born April 16, 1765.

Died April 5, 1833.

aged 68 years.

———

(Foot-stone.)

A. B.